D0944931

BY THOMAS K. ADAMSON

THE ARIZONA
CARDINALS
STORY

TORQUE
™

BELLWETHER MEDIA · MINNEAPOLIS, MN

Are you ready to take it to the extreme? Torque books thrust you into the action-packed world of sports, vehicles, mystery, and adventure. These books may include dirt, smoke, fire, and chilling tales. **WARNING** : read at your own risk.

This edition first published in 2017 by Bellwether Media, Inc.

No part of this publication may be reproduced in whole or in part without written permission of the publisher. For information regarding permission, write to Bellwether Media, Inc., Attention: Permissions Department, 5357 Penn Avenue South, Minneapolis, MN 55419.

Library of Congress Cataloging-in-Publication Data

Names: Adamson, Thomas K., 1970-
Title: The Arizona Cardinals Story / by Thomas K. Adamson.
Description: Minneapolis, MN : Bellwether Media, Inc., 2017. | Series:
   Torque: NFL Teams | Includes bibliographical references and index.
Identifiers: LCCN 2015038072 | ISBN 9781626173552 (hardcover : alk. paper)
Subjects: LCSH: Arizona Cardinals (Football team)–History–Juvenile literature.
Classification: LCC GV956.A75 A43 2017 | DDC 796.332/640979173–dc23
LC record available at http://lccn.loc.gov/2015038072

Printed in the United States of America, North Mankato, MN.

TABLE OF CONTENTS

On January 16, 2016, the Arizona Cardinals trail the Green Bay Packers by 3 points. The Cards need a fourth-quarter comeback.

Carson Palmer

Michael Floyd

Quarterback Carson Palmer throws to **wide receiver** Larry Fitzgerald. A defender tips the pass. Luckily, it lands in the arms of wide receiver Michael Floyd. Touchdown!

5

Larry Fitzgerald

Minutes later, the Cardinals also kick a field goal. Then a **Hail Mary** touchdown by Green Bay takes the game into overtime.

On the first play, Palmer finds Fitzgerald wide open. Fitzgerald breaks tackles to run 75 yards! Two plays later, he gets the ball to the end zone. It is a **playoff** win!

SCORING TERMS

END ZONE
the area at each end of a football field; a team scores by entering the opponent's end zone with the football.

EXTRA POINT
a score that occurs when a kicker kicks the ball between the opponent's goal posts after a touchdown is scored; 1 point.

FIELD GOAL
a score that occurs when a kicker kicks the ball between the opponent's goal posts; 3 points.

SAFETY
a score that occurs when a player on offense is tackled behind his own goal line; 2 points for defense.

TOUCHDOWN
a score that occurs when a team crosses into its opponent's end zone with the football; 6 points.

TWO-POINT CONVERSION
a score that occurs when a team crosses into its opponent's end zone with the football after scoring a touchdown; 2 points.

No National Football League (NFL) team is older than the Cardinals. The team has been around since 1898! Many things have changed over the years.

CARD-PITT
In 1944, many NFL players were fighting in World War II. The Chicago Cardinals combined with the Pittsburgh Steelers that year. They were called Card-Pitt.

Their name changed more than once. They moved from the Midwest to the Southwest. Recently in Arizona, the team has found success. They played in **Super Bowl** 43.

The Cardinals play their home games at University of Phoenix Stadium. The huge stadium in Glendale, Arizona, looks like a barrel cactus.

Its roof and field are both **retractable**. The natural grass field can be rolled outside to get sunlight and water. It is rolled back inside for games.

GLENDALE, ARIZONA

W + E
N
S

Many football fans in Arizona were Dallas Cowboys fans before the Cardinals moved to the state. This means the Cowboys are a big National Football **Conference** (NFC) **rival**.

Arizona's **division** rivals are the Los Angeles Rams, San Francisco 49ers, and Seattle Seahawks. All four teams belong to the NFC West.

NFL DIVISIONS

AFC

AFC NORTH

BALTIMORE **RAVENS**

CINCINNATI **BENGALS**

CLEVELAND **BROWNS**

PITTSBURGH **STEELERS**

AFC EAST

BUFFALO **BILLS**

MIAMI **DOLPHINS**

NEW ENGLAND **PATRIOTS**

NEW YORK **JETS**

AFC SOUTH

HOUSTON **TEXANS**

INDIANAPOLIS **COLTS**

JACKSONVILLE **JAGUARS**

TENNESSEE **TITANS**

AFC WEST

DENVER **BRONCOS**

KANSAS CITY **CHIEFS**

OAKLAND **RAIDERS**

SAN DIEGO **CHARGERS**

A WIN IN MEXICO

On October 2, 2005, the Cardinals beat the 49ers in Mexico City, Mexico. Playing a regular-season game in another country was an NFL first!

NFC

NFC NORTH

CHICAGO
BEARS

DETROIT
LIONS

GREEN BAY
PACKERS

MINNESOTA
VIKINGS

NFC EAST

DALLAS
COWBOYS

NEW YORK
GIANTS

PHILADELPHIA
EAGLES

WASHINGTON
REDSKINS

NFC SOUTH

ATLANTA
FALCONS

CAROLINA
PANTHERS

NEW ORLEANS
SAINTS

TAMPA BAY
BUCCANEERS

NFC WEST

ARIZONA
CARDINALS

LOS ANGELES
RAMS

SAN FRANCISCO
49ERS

SEATTLE
SEAHAWKS

The Cardinals are one of the original NFL teams. They helped **found** the NFL in 1920. They were based in Chicago, Illinois, at that time. Five years later, the Cardinals claimed the NFL Championship. Their last NFL Championship was in 1947. They defeated the Philadelphia Eagles to win the title.

RUN, CHARLEY!

Charley Trippi scored two touchdowns in the 1947 Championship game. One was a 75-yard punt return!

1947 WORLD CHAMPIONS
Charley Trippi
CHICAGO CARDINALS-28
PHILADELPHIA EAGLES-21

CHARLEY TRIPPI
PRO HALL OF FAME
INDUCTED 1968

GEORGIA
BULLDOG

1925 season

WINNING RECORD

In 1925, there were no playoffs. The Cardinals' record earned them the NFL Championship.

In 1960, the Cardinals moved to St. Louis, Missouri. Phoenix, Arizona, became their new home in 1988.

1970s in St. Louis

The team came close to a Super Bowl win following the 2008 season. They lost a well-played game to the Pittsburgh Steelers. After the 2015 season, the team made it to the NFC Championship game.

1898

Formed in Chicago as the Morgan Athletic Club

1920

Helped found the NFL

1947

Won the NFL Championship, beating the Philadelphia Eagles (28-21)

1960

Moved to Missouri to become the St. Louis Cardinals

1925

Claimed their first NFL Championship by having the league's best record (11 wins, 2 losses, 1 tie)

1948

Played in their second straight NFL Championship game, but lost to the Philadelphia Eagles (0-7)

2009

Played in Super Bowl 43, but lost to the Pittsburgh Steelers

23 FINAL SCORE **27**

1975

Claimed the division title for the second season in a row

1988

Moved to Arizona to become the Phoenix Cardinals

1994

Changed their name to the Arizona Cardinals

2015

Hired Jen Welter, the NFL's first female coach

Hall-of-Fame tackle Dan Dierdorf was a top protector of Cardinals quarterbacks. He made sure the team allowed the fewest **sacks** in the league more than once in the 1970s!

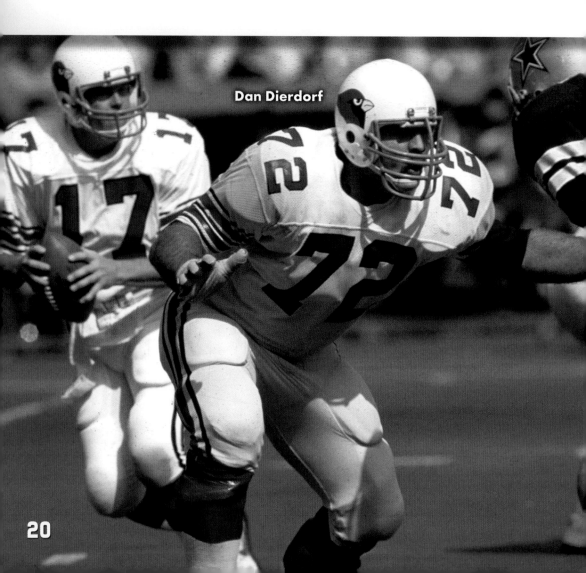

Dan Dierdorf

Ottis Anderson

In 1979, **running back** Ottis Anderson joined the team. He went on to become the team's all-time leading **rusher**. He ran for 7,999 yards!

For **defense**, Aeneas
Williams is viewed as one of
the best **cornerbacks** ever.
He holds the team record for
most **interception** returns
for a touchdown.

Wide receiver Larry
Fitzgerald holds team records
for total receptions and most
receiving yards. He was the
go-to guy for quarterback Kurt
Warner in Super Bowl 43.

TEAM GREATS

CHARLEY TRIPPI
HALFBACK, QUARTERBACK
1947-1955

DAN DIERDORF
OFFENSIVE TACKLE
1971-1983

OTTIS ANDERSON
RUNNING BACK
1979-1986

Aeneas Williams

AENEAS WILLIAMS
CORNERBACK
1991-2000

LARRY FITZGERALD
WIDE RECEIVER
2004-PRESENT

KURT WARNER
QUARTERBACK
2005-2009

SUN DEVIL STADIUM

When the Cardinals moved to Arizona, they did not have an instant fan base. At Sun Devil Stadium, they had some sellouts. But the packed crowds were usually Cowboys fans during games against Dallas.

The University of Phoenix Stadium and recent winning seasons have drawn new support. Today, the new stadium fills up with Cardinals fans.

The Cardinals started a loud home tradition in 2013. They brought in the Big Red Siren to get fans pumped up.

Big Red (mascot)

Big Red Siren

Each game, a famous guest cranks the siren
before the players are introduced. Former
Cardinals stars are often given this honor!

MORE ABOUT THE
CARDINALS

Team name:
Arizona Cardinals

Team name explained:
Named for faded maroon
jerseys that looked
cardinal red

Nickname: Cards

Joined NFL: 1920

Conference: NFC

Division: West

Main rivals: San Francisco 49ers,
Dallas Cowboys

Hometown:
Phoenix, Arizona

Training camp location:
University of Phoenix Stadium, Glendale, Arizona

ARIZONA

PHOENIX

N
W E
S

Home stadium name: University of Phoenix Stadium

Stadium opened: 2006

Seats in stadium: 63,400

Logo: The head of a cardinal

Colors: Cardinal red, black, white

Mascot: Big Red

GLOSSARY

conference—a large grouping of sports teams that often play one another

cornerbacks—players on defense whose main job is to stop wide receivers from catching passes; a cornerback is positioned outside of the linebackers.

defense—the group of players who try to stop the opposing team from scoring

division—a small grouping of sports teams that often play one another; usually there are several divisions of teams in a conference.

found—to start a team, company, or other group

Hail Mary—a last-second long pass play at the end of a game

interception—a catch made by a defensive player of a pass thrown by the opposing team

playoff—a game played after the regular NFL season is over; playoff games determine which teams play in the Super Bowl.

quarterback—a player on offense whose main job is to throw and hand off the ball

retractable—able to be moved somewhere and then pulled back

rival—a long-standing opponent

running back—a player on offense whose main job is to run with the ball

rusher—a player who runs with the ball

sacks—plays during which a player on defense tackles the opposing quarterback for a loss of yards

Super Bowl—the championship game for the NFL

wide receiver—a player on offense whose main job is to catch passes from the quarterback

TO LEARN MORE

AT THE LIBRARY

Monnig, Alex. *Arizona Cardinals.* Mankato, Minn.: Child's World, 2015.

Sandler, Michael. *Larry Fitzgerald.* New York, N.Y.: Bearport Pub., 2010.

Wyner, Zach. *Arizona Cardinals.* New York, N.Y.: AV2 by Weigl, 2014.

ON THE WEB

Learning more about the Arizona Cardinals is as easy as 1, 2, 3.

1. Go to www.factsurfer.com.

2. Enter "Arizona Cardinals" into the search box.

3. Click the "Surf" button and you will see a list of related web sites.

With factsurfer.com, finding more information is just a click away.

INDEX

The images in this book are reproduced through the courtesy of: Corbis, front cover (large, small), pp. 10-11, 11, 16, 16-17; Mark J. Rebilas/ USA Today Sports/ Newscom, pp. 4-5; Paul Spinelli/ AP Images, pp. 5, 7, 23 (middle); Roy Dabner/ EPA/ Newscom, pp. 6-7; Henry Romero/ Reuters/ Newscom, pp. 12-13; Deposit Photos/ Glow Images, pp. 12-13 (logos), 18-19 (logos), 28-29 (logos); John Bazemore/ AP Images, p. 14; Pro Football Hall of Fame/ AP Images, pp. 15, 18 (top, bottom left); AP Images, p. 18 (bottom right); ZUMA Press/ Alamy, pp. 19 (top right), 28; NFL Photos/ AP Images, pp. 19 (top left), 22, 23 (right); Matt York/ AP Images, p. 19 (bottom); David Durochik/ AP Images, pp. 20-21; Vernon Biever/ AP Images, p. 21; Ron Cortes/ KRT/ Newscom, pp. 22-23; David Stluka/ AP Images, p. 23 (right); Derrick Neill, p. 24; Cal Sport Media/ Alamy, p. 25; David J. Phillip/ AP Images, p. 26; Christian Petersen/ Getty Images, pp. 26-27; Ron Niebrugge/ Alamy, p. 29 (stadium); Darryll Webb/ Reuters/ Newscom, p. 29 (mascot).